NFL's TOP 10
TEAMS

by Will Graves

NFL's TOP TEN

SportsZone
An Imprint of Abdo Publishing
abdopublishing.com

abdopublishing.com

Published by Abdo Publishing, a division of ABDO, PO Box 398166, Minneapolis, Minnesota 55439. Copyright © 2018 by Abdo Consulting Group, Inc. International copyrights reserved in all countries. No part of this book may be reproduced in any form without written permission from the publisher. SportsZone™ is a trademark and logo of Abdo Publishing.

Printed in the United States of America, North Mankato, Minnesota
042017
092017

THIS BOOK CONTAINS
RECYCLED MATERIALS

Cover Photo: Arthur Anderson/AP Images
Interior Photos: Michael Conroy/AP Images, 4–5; Bettmann/Getty Images, 7; NFL Photos/AP Images, 9; Al Messerschmidt/AP Images, 8–9, 27; Tony Tomsic/AP Images, 10, 11, 23, 25; Doug Mills/AP Images, 12–13; Paul Spinelli/AP Images, 15; Lynda Kaye/AP Images, 17; John W. McDonough/Icon Sportswire, 16–17; Arthur Anderson/AP Images, 18–19; AP Images, 20, 26; David Durochik/AP Images, 21; Mark Foley/AP Images, 24

Editor: Patrick Donnelly
Series Designer: Craig Hinton

Publisher's Cataloging-in-Publication Data

Names: Graves, Will, author.
Title: NFL's top 10 teams / by Will Graves.
Other titles: NFL's top ten teams
Description: Minneapolis, MN : Abdo Publishing, 2018. | Series: NFL's top ten |
    Includes bibliographical references and index.
Identifiers: LCCN 2016963097 | ISBN 9781532111440 (lib. bdg.) |
    ISBN 9781680789294 (ebook)
Subjects: LCSH: National Football League--Juvenile literature. | Football--
    --United States--history--Juvenile literature. | Football--United States--
    Miscellanea--Juvenile literature. | Football--United States--Statistics--Juvenile
    literature.
Classification: DDC 796.332--dc23
LC record available at http://lccn.loc.gov/2016963097

Table of
CONTENTS

Introduction

Every National Football League (NFL) season ends with one team dancing in confetti, passing around the Lombardi Trophy after winning the Super Bowl.

However, not all winners are created equal. The best of the best find a way to do more than just outscore their opponents. They dominate. Some do it with defense. Some do it with offense. Some do it with Hall of Fame coaches. Some do it with game-changing players.

Each team arrives in training camp every summer dreaming of winning it all. And every year one team does.

Every once in a while, something special happens. Every once in a while, a team goes beyond simply winning the Super Bowl and leaves the kind of lasting legacy reserved for legends.

Let's meet the best teams in NFL history.

10

Jubilant Chicago Bears players celebrate their second straight NFL title after throttling the New York Giants in 1941.

1941 Chicago Bears

George Halas played and coached for the Chicago Bears for a decade before retiring after the 1929 season. But his retirement did not last long. The Bears lured Halas back in 1933 to serve as head coach, a move that ranks as one of the smartest in NFL history.

By 1940 the Bears were among the league's best, thanks in part to the play of star quarterback Sid Luckman. But Washington Redskins owner George Preston Marshall wasn't a fan. He called the Bears crybabies after his team edged Chicago 7–3 late in the 1940 regular season.

When the teams played in the NFL Championship Game a few weeks later, Halas reminded his players of Marshall's comments. The result was a 73–0 Bears victory that remains the most lopsided score in any NFL game.

That triumph served as a launching pad for an even more dominant season in 1941. The Bears went 10–1 during the regular season. Their only defeat came in a 16–14 loss to Green Bay in early November. Luckman led all NFL quarterbacks in passer rating, and the Bears had the top rushing and passing attack in the league.

The Bears and Packers tied for the Western Division title, forcing a playoff game at Chicago's Soldier Field. George McAfee rushed for 119 yards, and Norm Standlee scored two touchdowns as Chicago won easily, 33–14. The next week, the Bears smashed the New York Giants 37–9

to win the NFL title. Standlee again scored twice, Luckman was 9-for-12 passing for 160 yards, and the defense held the Giants to just 157 total yards.

The "Monsters of the Midway," as the Bears became known, were born.

9

1991 Washington Redskins

Some champions build their teams around a star quarterback. The Washington Redskins under coach Joe Gibbs took a very different path. They focused on "the Hogs."

Washington won three Super Bowls with three different quarterbacks between 1982 and 1991. Three key members of the Hogs—the team's offensive linemen—were there through it all.

Their actual names were Joe Jacoby, Russ Grimm, and Jeff Bostic. Offensive line coach Joe Bugel began calling them the Hogs, in part because they were all big guys. Their average weight was 285 pounds in a time when most linemen were significantly smaller.

The Hogs helped clear the way to Super Bowl titles in the 1982 and 1987 seasons. But their finest hour came in the 1991 season. Washington rolled through the regular season, averaging an NFL-best 30.3 points per game on the way to a 14–2 record.

Quarterback Mark Rypien threw for 28 touchdowns that year on his way to making the Pro Bowl. But the guys who played

GROUP PARTICIPATION

The Hogs weren't the only Washington players with a catchy nickname. Wide receivers Gary Clark, Ricky Sanders, and Art Monk called themselves "the Posse." The trio combined for 23 touchdown catches in 1991.

The Hogs did a great job of protecting Mark Rypien, *11*.

in front of him deserved a lot of credit. Rypien attempted 427 passes in 1991. He was sacked only seven times.

The playoffs brought more of the same. Rypien wasn't sacked once as Washington whipped the Atlanta Falcons, the Detroit Lions, and the Buffalo Bills on the way to its third Super Bowl in a decade.

The Hogs changed the way football teams thought about offensive linemen. These days most NFL rosters are filled with linemen who weigh more than 300 pounds.

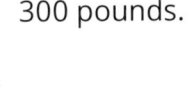

8

Bart Starr drops back
to pass in the first
Super Bowl.

1966 Green Bay Packers

The Green Bay Packers won the NFL championship in 1961, 1962, and 1965. But 1966 brought a new challenge. Being the best in the NFL was no longer good enough. The rival American Football League (AFL) had begun play in 1960. It proved so successful the two leagues planned to merge in 1970.

First, however, the leagues arranged a game that pitted the champions of each league against each other. Today that game is called the Super Bowl.

The Packers wanted to be the first to represent the NFL. They left little doubt while going 12–2 during the 1966 season. Quarterback Bart Starr was the league's highest-rated passer, while the Packers defense held opponents to 11.6 points per game.

Green Bay edged the Dallas Cowboys in the NFL title game. That set up a meeting with the AFL champion Kansas City Chiefs

Max McGee hauls in one of his two touchdown receptions on the day.

BACK TO BACK FOR PACK

The Packers weren't done winning under Lombardi. They beat the Oakland Raiders in the second Super Bowl before he walked away from coaching in Green Bay. Lombardi's influence lives on. The winner of the Super Bowl now receives the Vince Lombardi Trophy.

at the Los Angeles Coliseum in the first Super Bowl. Packers coach Vince Lombardi didn't think the new league was the NFL's equal, and he wanted to beat the Chiefs to prove his point.

The Packers did, and then some. Veteran wide receiver Max McGee was pressed into playing when starter Boyd Dowler left with a broken leg. McGee caught two touchdown passes and Elijah Pitts ran for two scores as Green Bay pulled away in the second half for a 35–10 win.

After the game, Lombardi said he didn't think the Chiefs measured up to the best teams in the NFL. No team that season, and few ever, measured up to the 1966 Packers. Lombardi and 10 of his players ended up in the Pro Football Hall of Fame, and their success earned Green Bay the nickname "Titletown USA."

7

John Elway, *left*, and the Broncos kept the rest of the league at arm's length throughout the 1998 season.

1998 Denver Broncos

John Elway spent the prime of his Hall of Fame career on teams not quite good enough to win it all. Three times between the 1986 and 1989 seasons, the Denver Broncos quarterback led his team to the Super Bowl. The Broncos were crushed in all three games.

Eventually Elway got some help. In 1997 running back Terrell Davis, a raw talent drafted in the sixth round, became one of the best players in the NFL. Davis was named the Super Bowl Most Valuable Player (MVP) as the Broncos upset the defending champion Green Bay Packers.

The victory was vindication for Elway, but he wanted more. The Broncos spent the 1998 season proving their victory over Green Bay was no fluke. With Elway sidelined by injury for four games, the Broncos relied heavily on Davis, who became the fourth running back in league history to run for more than 2,000 yards. He finished with 2,008 rushing yards and was named the NFL MVP.

The Broncos flirted with perfection. They won their first 13 games before losing to the New York Giants and the Miami Dolphins. But those setbacks were temporary. Denver crushed Miami in a playoffs rematch and put away the New York Jets to reach the Super Bowl, where the upstart Atlanta Falcons awaited.

The final contest was no contest. Denver dominated Atlanta on its way to a 34–19 win. The player once criticized for his Super Bowl failures ended his 16-year career by cementing his status among the greats. Elway threw for 336 yards and a touchdown while being named the game's MVP.

Elway exited to a standing ovation with a minute to play. He pulled his helmet off and saluted the roaring crowd as Denver became the seventh team to win back-to-back Super Bowls.

6

Patriots quarterback
Tom Brady shook off
an illness to beat the
Pittsburgh Steelers in the
AFC Championship Game. →

2004 New England Patriots

Tom Brady led the 2001 New England Patriots on a stunning run to the playoffs. It ended with an upset of the St. Louis Rams in the Super Bowl. But that was just the start for the Patriots. They won it all again in the 2003 season, beating the Carolina Panthers in the Super Bowl on Adam Vinatieri's last-second field goal.

That team, however, relied heavily on its defense to win. In 2004 Brady and the offense finally caught up.

Brady passed for 28 touchdowns on his way to the Pro Bowl as the Patriots went 14–2. The defense assembled by coach Bill Belichick was nasty and versatile. At one point, injuries forced New England to use wide receiver Troy Brown as a defensive back. Brown responded by intercepting three passes on the season.

The run to another title hit one major speed bump on the eve of the American Football Conference (AFC) Championship Game. The Patriots were in Pittsburgh to face the Steelers. Pittsburgh had handed the Patriots their first loss of the year on Halloween. Brady spent the night before the playoff game with a 103-degree fever and needed to have fluids given to him through a needle in his arm.

It barely slowed him down. Playing in frigid weather, Brady threw for 207 yards and two touchdowns as New England raced to a 24–3 halftime lead. The Patriots held on for a 41–27 victory. Then they outlasted the Philadelphia Eagles 24–21 in the Super Bowl. Brady passed for two touchdowns as New England became just the second team to win three Super Bowls in four seasons.

Michael Irvin signals a Dallas first down in a 1993 game. ↓

1993 Dallas Cowboys

They were called "the Triplets." Troy Aikman, Emmitt Smith, and Michael Irvin brought back memories of the Dallas Cowboys' glory days of the 1970s. When Jerry Jones bought the Cowboys in 1989, he hired brash University of Miami coach Jimmy Johnson to begin a drastic makeover. Over the course of the next three years, Johnson laid the foundation for a turnaround that made history.

Irvin, a high-flying wide receiver, was already in the fold when Johnson took over. The Cowboys selected Aikman, a star quarterback, with the first pick in the 1989 NFL Draft. A year later, the hard-running Smith arrived, completing the trio. They gave the Cowboys one of the most talented quarterback/wide receiver/running back combinations the league had ever seen.

Dallas rose to power quickly. The Cowboys won the Super Bowl after the 1992 season, embarrassing the Buffalo Bills 52–17. The 1993 season started with Smith holding out for a new contract. After Dallas lost its first two games of the

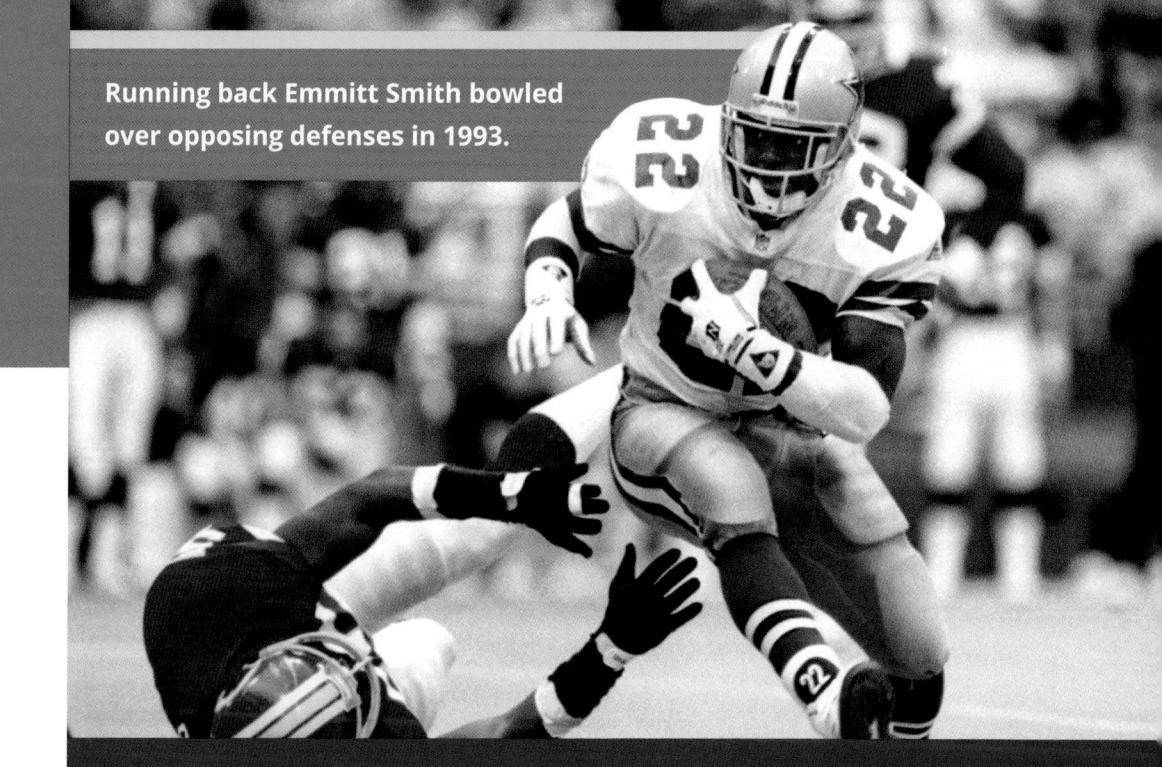

Running back Emmitt Smith bowled over opposing defenses in 1993.

HIT THE ROAD, JIMMY

Even though he'd built the Cowboys into winners, Johnson did not stick around. He had a falling out with Jones after the Super Bowl. Dallas hired former University of Oklahoma coach Barry Switzer, and the Triplets captured a third Super Bowl after the 1995 season.

season, Smith signed a deal that made him the highest-paid running back in the league.

With the Triplets reunited, Dallas went on a tear. The Cowboys lost just twice the rest of the way, capturing their second straight Super Bowl in a rematch with the Bills. Smith proved to be the difference, running for 132 yards and two second-half touchdowns as Dallas rallied for a 30–13 win.

4

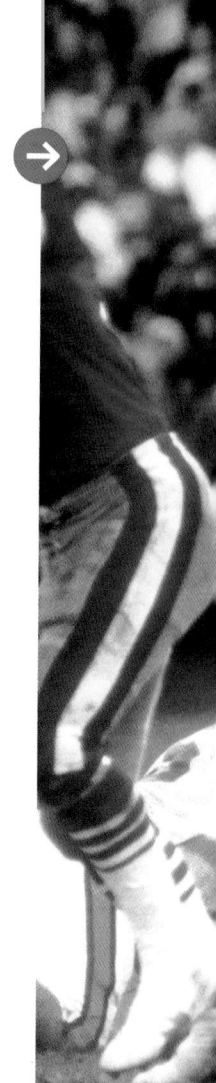

The 49ers had success using Roger Craig, *center*, in a variety of ways.

1984 San Francisco 49ers

Coach Bill Walsh and quarterback Joe Montana turned the San Francisco 49ers into winners using a system known as the West Coast Offense in the early 1980s. It relied on short, accurate passes that let receivers run free after the catch. The quarterback called "Joe Cool" worked it to near perfection.

The 49ers won their first Super Bowl after the 1981 season, but they were a Cinderella story that year. By 1984 they were a powerhouse that overwhelmed opponents on both sides of the ball. Running back Roger Craig was a versatile weapon who caught 71 passes out of the backfield. The offensive line gave Montana all the time he needed to go to work, and three of the linemen reached the Pro Bowl.

While the offense received the majority of the attention, the defense was even better. Led by hard-hitting safety Ronnie Lott, the 49ers allowed the fewest points in the NFL. San Francisco became the first team ever to go 15–1 in the regular season. The 49ers cruised to the Super Bowl, holding off the New York Giants and shutting out the Chicago Bears in the playoffs.

In the Super Bowl, Craig set a record by scoring three touchdowns. But the real story was the San Francisco defense. The 49ers sent a message to record-setting Miami Dolphins quarterback Dan Marino and his high-flying offense: the San Francisco defense was a no-passing zone. The 49ers intercepted Marino twice and shut out the Dolphins in the second half of a 38–16 victory.

3

Terry Bradshaw starred in the Super Bowl against the Dallas Cowboys.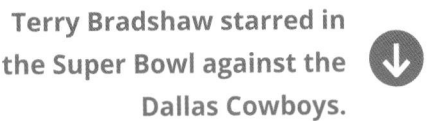

1978 Pittsburgh Steelers

The Pittsburgh Steelers won back-to-back Super Bowls after the 1974 and 1975 seasons behind a defense known as "the Steel Curtain." Led by defensive end "Mean" Joe Greene and tenacious linebacker Jack Lambert, the Steelers played a physical, bruising style of football that wore opponents down.

By the late 1970s, though, the NFL was changing. The league adjusted its rules to make it easier for offenses to score. Rather than complain, Pittsburgh decided to get with the times. For years the Steelers offense was built around running backs Franco Harris and Rocky Bleier. Coach Chuck Noll often asked quarterback Terry Bradshaw to simply avoid mistakes while Harris, Bleier, and the defense went to work.

But under the new, offense-friendly rules, Bradshaw proved he could win games with his arm. Pittsburgh stormed through the 1978 regular season with a 14–2 record. Bradshaw was named the NFL MVP after throwing a

Jack Lambert, *58*, and the Steel Curtain defense dominated foes throughout the 1970s.

career-high 28 touchdown passes. Eleven of them went to acrobatic wide receiver Lynn Swann, while lightning-fast John Stallworth caught nine. Harris added 1,082 rushing yards and eight touchdowns.

After crushing the Denver Broncos and the Houston Oilers in the playoffs, a familiar foe awaited in the Super Bowl: the Dallas Cowboys. The Steelers had edged the Cowboys 21–17 in the big game three years earlier. The rematch was just as thrilling. Bradshaw made up for an early fumble that gave the Cowboys the lead by throwing for 318 yards and four touchdowns. The Steelers won 35–31, the third of their four Super Bowl victories in the 1970s.

Defensive coordinator
Buddy Ryan gets a ride off
the field after the Bears
won the Super Bowl.

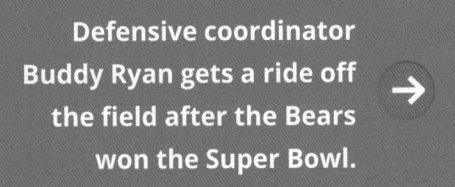

1985 Chicago Bears

The 1985 Chicago Bears were a confident bunch. And they had plenty of reasons to be optimistic about their chances on the field. Running back Walter Payton was already the NFL's all-time leading rusher, and at age 31 he was still an effective weapon for the Bears offense. Flashy quarterback Jim McMahon called the shots. The offense would even bring in rookie 335-pound nose tackle William "the Refrigerator" Perry to run the ball near the goal line.

But the heart of the 1985 Bears was its defense. Defensive coordinator Buddy Ryan devised what he called the "46" defense. It was designed to create as much pressure on opposing quarterbacks as possible. And it worked to perfection. The Bears didn't simply win games in 1985—they put on a show. The defense set an NFL record for fewest points allowed in a 16-game season while leading the league with 64 sacks and 55 forced turnovers.

Chicago won its first 12 games before stumbling in a 38–24 loss to the Miami Dolphins. The setback only seemed to make the Bears play harder. They shut out the New York Giants and the Los Angeles Rams in the playoffs, then blasted the New England Patriots 46–10 in the Super Bowl. It was the biggest blowout in Super Bowl history at the time. The Bears celebrated by carrying head coach Mike Ditka and Ryan off the field on their shoulders.

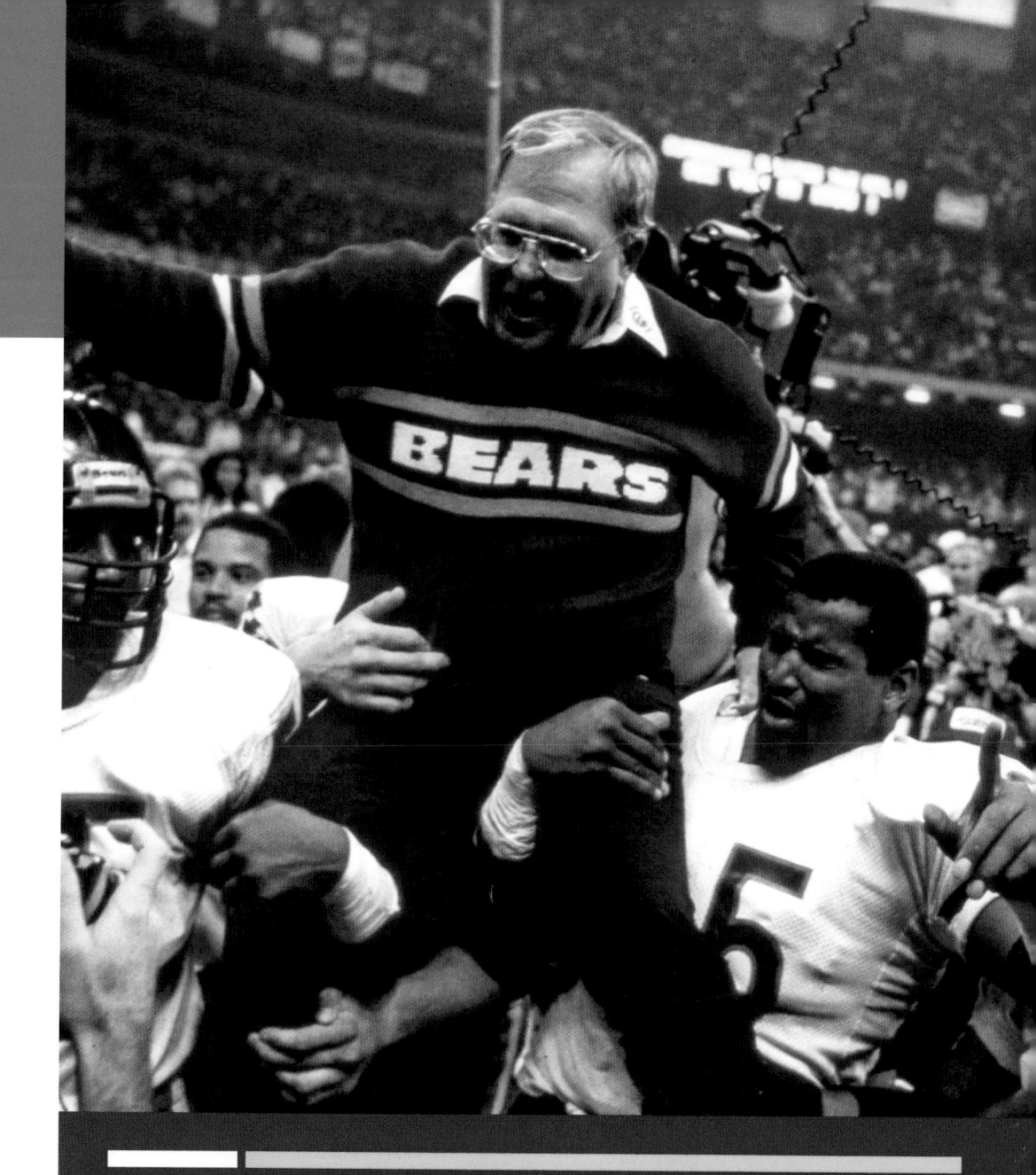

NO REPEAT PERFORMANCE

Chicago's defense was even better in 1986, giving up just 187 points, a record for fewest points allowed in a 16-game season. But McMahon was injured late in the year, and the Bears lost to Washington in the playoffs.

1

Don Shula poses between Earl Morrall, *left*, and Bob Griese. Both quarterbacks would play big roles in Miami's undefeated season.

1972 Miami Dolphins

The seeds of perfection were planted in defeat. The Miami Dolphins were a team on the rise in 1971. Coach Don Shula had needed just two seasons to turn the young expansion team into contenders after coming over from the Baltimore Colts. Miami made the playoffs for the first time in 1970 and reached its first Super Bowl the next season.

That's where Miami's luck ran out. The Dallas Cowboys pushed the Dolphins around in a 24–3 victory. The loss stung Shula, who already had to live down another Super Bowl defeat. His dominant 1968 Colts team

From left, Jim Kiick, Larry Csonka, and Mercury Morris take a break during the 1972 AFC Championship Game.

had fallen to the New York Jets in one of the sport's greatest upsets. After losing to the Cowboys, Shula was stuck with the reputation as a good coach who couldn't win the big one.

Over the course of the next year, everything changed. Shula told his players to keep the loss to the Cowboys close in their minds. In his house, cornerback Tim Foley hung a picture of the scoreboard showing the final score as a way to keep him motivated. By the time the Dolphins arrived for training camp in the summer of 1972, they had developed the winning edge Shula told them they needed to become champions.

Having some pretty great players also helped. The backfield featured quarterback Bob Griese and three running backs with three different styles. Larry Csonka was the bruising fullback. Halfback Mercury Morris had the speed to race past defenders. The versatile Jim Kiick was a great blocker and receiver.

The Miami defense was even better. The group led by linebacker Nick Buonoconti and defensive end Manny Fernandez didn't have a lot of stars. They picked up the nickname the "No-Name Defense" when Cowboys coach Tom Landry couldn't recall any of their names before the Super Bowl. By the end of the next season, the whole world knew who they were.

The road to history in 1972 hit a big detour along the way. Griese broke his leg in Week 5. Veteran Earl Morrall took over, and the Dolphins didn't miss a beat. The weeks went by and the Dolphins kept winning. There were some close calls, including a 24–23 escape against the Buffalo Bills in Week 6. The Dolphins needed a late touchdown run by Morris to nip the Jets 28–24 in Week 10.

Miami finished the regular season 14–0, but the offense looked out of sorts in the playoffs. They needed a fourth-quarter touchdown run by Kiick to get past the Cleveland Browns 20–14. They were tied 7–7 at halftime of the conference championship game against the Pittsburgh Steelers. That's when Shula decided to bench Morrall and give the now-healed Griese his job back. Like every other button Shula pushed that year, it worked. Trailing 10–7 early in the third quarter, the Dolphins rallied for a 21–17 win.

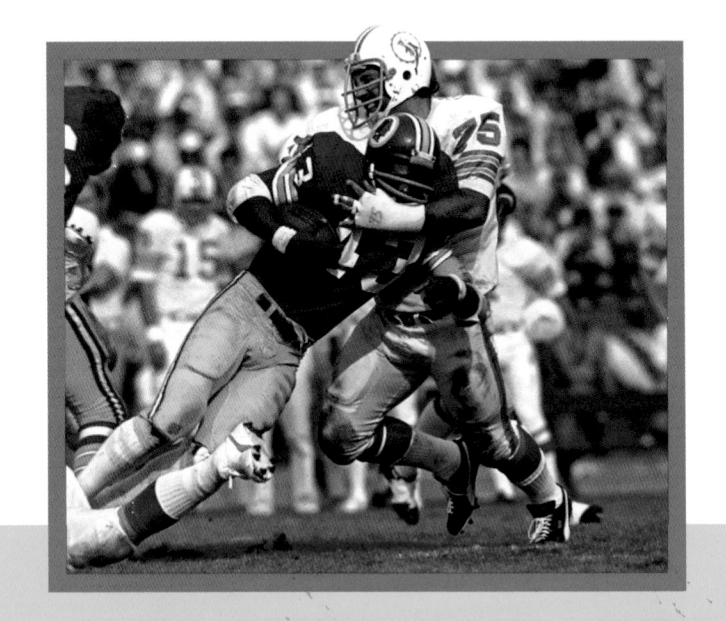

Miami defensive end Manny Fernandez wraps up Washington's Larry Brown in the Super Bowl.

BACK-TO-BACK TITLES

Shula and the Dolphins were back in the Super Bowl after the 1973 season. They hadn't gone undefeated again, but their 12–2 record was the best in the AFC. They cruised through the playoffs with comfortable wins over the Cincinnati Bengals and the Oakland Raiders. Then they crushed the Minnesota Vikings 24–7 in the Super Bowl to become the first team since the Green Bay Packers to win consecutive NFL championships.

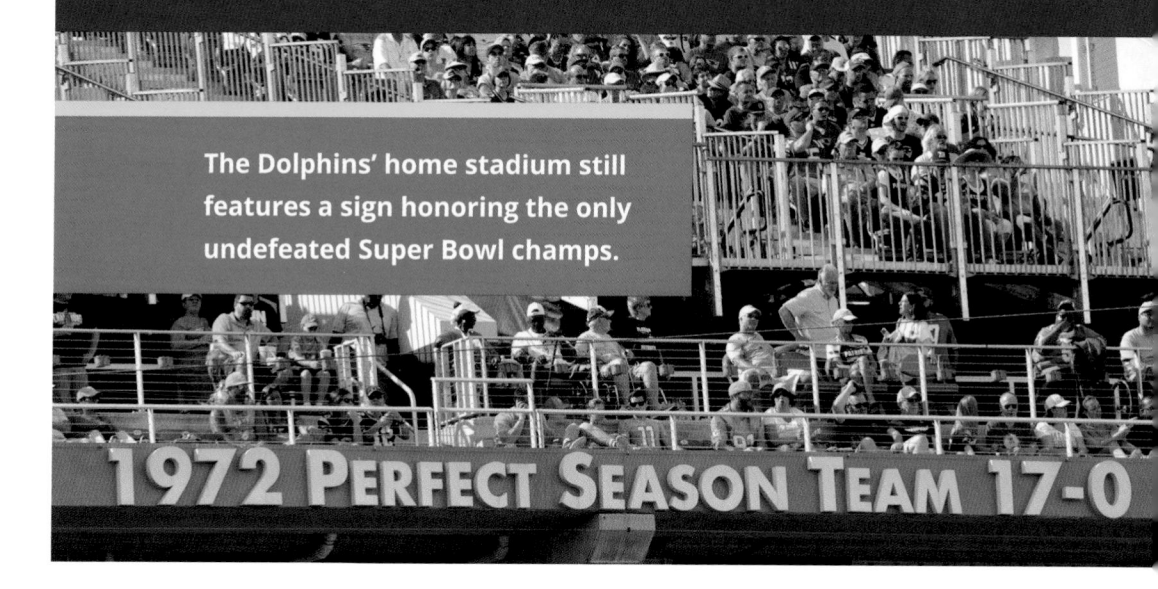

The Dolphins' home stadium still features a sign honoring the only undefeated Super Bowl champs.

1972 PERFECT SEASON TEAM 17-0

One more obstacle between Miami and 17–0 awaited: the Washington Redskins. The Dolphins handled them the way they beat every other team they faced in 1972. They used their stout defense and solid running game, and they avoided mistakes. Safety Jake Scott, leader of the Miami secondary, intercepted two passes in the 14–7 win. Scott was named the game's MVP, but there was little doubt that the real victory belonged to Shula.

The Dolphins players hoisted their coach onto their shoulders and carried him off the field and into history. The coach who couldn't win the big one had finally won it all.

Honorable Mentions

1950 CLEVELAND BROWNS: The Browns made quite the impression in their first NFL season, going 12–2 and beating the Los Angeles Rams on a late field goal by Lou Groza for the league title. The Browns had won four straight titles in the All-America Football Conference before they joined the NFL in 1950.

1976 OAKLAND RAIDERS: After years of playing second fiddle to Pittsburgh and Miami in the AFC, the Raiders broke through by going 13–1 and demolishing the Minnesota Vikings in the Super Bowl. Quarterback Ken "the Snake" Stabler teamed with wide receivers Cliff Branch and Fred Biletnikoff and tight end Dave Casper to shred opposing defenses.

1977 DALLAS COWBOYS: Rookie running back Tony Dorsett proved to be the missing piece to get the Cowboys over the Super Bowl hump after several years of close calls. Dorsett rushed for 1,007 yards and 12 touchdowns, while Randy White and Harvey Martin led a defense that posted 53 sacks.

1986 NEW YORK GIANTS: The Giants captured their first Super Bowl behind fiery coach Bill Parcells and a defense that featured Hall of Fame linebacker Lawrence Taylor. They went 14–2 in the regular season, then outscored three playoff opponents 105–23.

1996 GREEN BAY PACKERS: Quarterback Brett Favre and defensive end Reggie White restored "Titletown USA" to its rightful place in Green Bay as the NFL's top offense and top defense helped the Packers to their first Super Bowl win in nearly 30 years. Favre led the league with 39 touchdown passes, and the defense forced 39 turnovers.

1999 ST. LOUIS RAMS: Quarterback Kurt Warner, a 28-year-old rookie whose best games had come in arena football, was thrust into the starting role when Trent Green injured his knee in a preseason game. All Warner did was lead the "Greatest Show on Turf" to an NFL record for points on the way to edging the Tennessee Titans in the Super Bowl.

2000 BALTIMORE RAVENS: Their offense wasn't anything special, but the Ravens built a defense for the ages. Linebacker Ray Lewis and safety Rod Woodson led a talented, hard-hitting crew that gave up just 165 points and 970 rushing yards all season. In four playoff games the Ravens allowed just one offensive touchdown. Baltimore cruised to its first Super Bowl title with a 34–7 rout of the New York Giants.

2007 NEW ENGLAND PATRIOTS: Tom Brady and the Patriots were almost perfect in 2007. New England stormed into the Super Bowl with an 18–0 record, but its bid to join the perfect 1972 Dolphins ended with a 17–10 loss to the New York Giants.

Glossary

draft

A system that allows teams to acquire new players coming into a league.

expansion team

A new team that is added to an existing league.

legacy

Something of importance that came from someone in the past.

merge

Join with another to create something new, such as a company, a team, or a league.

playoffs

A set of games played after the regular season that decides which team is the champion.

roster

A list of players who make up a team.

sack

A tackle of the quarterback behind the line of scrimmage before he can pass the ball.

secondary

The defensive players— cornerbacks and safeties—who start the play farthest from the line.

upset

When a supposedly weaker team beats a stronger team.

For More Information

Books

Anastasio, Dina. *What Is the Super Bowl?* New York: Grosset & Dunlap, 2015.

Bryant, Howard. *Legends: The Best Players, Games, and Teams in Football.* New York: Philomel Books, 2015.

Editors of Sports Illustrated for Kids. *Sports Illustrated Kids 1st and 10: Top 10 Lists of Everything in Football.* New York: Sports Illustrated, 2016.

Websites

To learn more about the NFL, visit **abdobooklinks.com**. These links are routinely monitored and updated to provide the most current information available.

Place to Visit

Pro Football Hall of Fame

2121 George Halas Drive NW
Canton, Ohio 44708
330-456-8207
www.profootballhof.com

The Hall of Fame is like a museum dedicated to football. There are exhibits on the origins of the game, artifacts from famous moments, and busts honoring the greatest players and coaches ever.

Index

About the Author

Will Graves has spent the last 20 years as a sportswriter, covering professional sports and the Olympics. He is also the author of more than a dozen children's sports books. He currently works for the Associated Press in Pittsburgh, Pennsylvania, where he lives with his wife and two kids.